Leadership Lessons...Proven on the Front Line

Beverly Fortenberry

Acknowledgements

Thanks to Joni Fisher who provided guidance in writing this book and to all my colleagues who felt I had something worthwhile to say.

Table of Contents

Introduction

Leaders and managers who are able to make decisions on what to do and how to do it on the spot—in real time—are the ones who tend to survive and thrive in business. They draw from their experience the right principle or method to use to get the most effective result.

But no one ever builds their leadership and management principles and methods based solely on their own experiences. Most of what we know we have learned from listening to and watching others. This is why these stories can be so helpful because they have been the experiences of managers on the front line.

The lessons can be helpful to both the seasoned manager as well as the novice. Seasoned managers will be able to affirm actions that have led to their success and identify actions that some of their newer managers need to learn. These new managers will find this collection will help them in building a sound management foundation.

Today, more than ever, companies and their managers need to be fast, agile, and able to think and decide in real time. Wise managers continually look for opportunities to add to their experience base, challenging themselves to identify the critical few principles and actions that, if fine-tuned, will make a significant impact on their future success.

I gathered these stories over the 35 years I have worked in business and education. Some examples just stuck in my brain because of what the managers did to sabotage their careers. I noted others because they provided a role model of a really good management practice. Initially, I jotted down these incidents to share with my clients and colleagues. Finally, at their urging I compiled them to share with others.

No matter what business or profession you are in, you will find these stories fit. I hope you enjoy reading them and that you use the application questions that follow each story to reflect on how they might apply in your world of work.

The Management Mountain

Think of a business as a mountain. The leaders of the business reside at its summit. From their vantage point, they have a 360-degree view of what's happening around them. They can see a potential ambush from a competitor, a possible flood of new government legislation, opportunities for acquiring new markets. Armed with their comprehensive view they must act on how such events will affect the business.

In well-run companies, leaders set up communication channels to send information down the mountain to each level of management and staff. These channels of communication are extremely important because the more people are aware of challenges and opportunities the more they can feel involved and ready to protect their mountain.

Equally important is the fact that at each descending level of the mountain, the managers' view at that level of impending danger and opportunity narrows. They don't have the vantage point of being able to see it all. Each manager sees only his or her part of the mountain, yet they are responsible for clarifying all the news to their employees.

So, it is that each manager is responsible for providing the widest possible perspective from his or her vantage point on the mountain. The more employees can see the same view from their place on the mountain that the leaders see, the more they will feel a part of the company.

A few years ago, a Southern regional bank had a CEO who used his 'elevator time' to see if his managers were engaging in this type of communication. He was known to ask employees, on the elevator with him, questions about the banks vision and goals and most importantly why these were important to the company. If he liked what he heard, he would say, "That's why we should be proud to be working for our company." If he didn't like what he heard, he'd find out who their manager was and have a little talk with them. This CEO knew it all starts at the top.

Application Questions

1. How does your company communicate its goals, strategies, challenges and opportunities to managers and employees?
2. How often does this occur?
3. How do you share information with your team?
4. What form does this communication take? (meetings, emails, memos, etc)
5. How often does this occur?
6. How do you confirm or validate your understanding of information communicated to you?
7. What do you do to follow up on information you share with your team?
8. What could you do to improve communications with your team?

The Price Tag of Success

Moving up has costs attached. These costs will vary depending on the way the business is organized and how managers are used. In some companies managers' functions may be focused strategically or tactically so a manager may have part of the overall job of being a manager. In other organizations, managers have both aspects of the position and the company may have written detailed procedural manuals for managers.

Some companies routinely rotate managers to build experiences and management bench strength. This creates learning opportunities and challenges for new managers who frequently have less experience than those they manage.

Regardless of the situation, the new position will cost you in time, in effort to learn new skills, and sometimes even in personal changes, locations and relationships. One of the hidden costs that you must pay is the cost of leaping from the security of the 'known' where you were successful to the 'unknown' where you have no proven track record.

You might also experience fear that your successor might ruin what you had accomplished or, even worse, do it better than you did. Still, unless your successor reports to you, you can't be involved in doing both jobs.

So, if you plan to move up in management, know that you'll pay a price to get there and that you will have to leave behind much of what made you eligible for promotion in the first place. Consider this an 'opportunity cost'.

Application Questions

1. If you are going to promote someone to a position in an area they are unfamiliar with:
   - What specific expectations regarding their new position are you going to share with them?
   - How do you want them to introduce themselves to their new team?
   - How much authority are you planning to give them? How will you explain this to them?
   - What do you hope they do to learn from the team?
   - How do you plan to work with them once the move has occurred?

2. If you are being promoted to a position in which you have little to no experience (you are being rotated as per company policy or you are new to the company):
   - What research have you done on the business unit and the people on the team? (tasks, measures and tracking, successes, people skills)
   - How do you plan to introduce yourself and your experience?
   - How do you plan to work with the team and learn from them?
   - How do you plan to communicate with the team? How often?
   - How do you plan to reciprocate for any help the team members give you in teaching and coaching you in the new processes and procedures?

As Others See It

Imagine a valley with a river running through it. It is a light-filled spring day. Three artists, Van Gogh, Picasso and Cezanne arrive. They set up their easels and paint the scene. They all see exactly the same thing, or do they?

Imagine a city street at night. A thief accosts a young man coming out of a building. He steals the man's briefcase and runs away. Three writers, Grisham, Faulkner and Hemingway, observe the scene from their respective apartment windows. Each uses the event as the basis for a short story. Their stories tell the same tale don't they?

Each of us sees the world and its events from the perspective of our experiences. What we have learned shapes how we interpret what we see. Because our views are unique to us, the actions we take in a similar situation frequently will differ.

The manager who seeks to learn how others see things adds to his own view point, enabling him or her to see farther and wider than before. By sharing viewpoints, we expand our perspectives and make better decisions.

Application Questions

1. How open are you to others ideas, opinions and suggestions?
2. What do you usually do with other peoples perceptions? Do you:
    - Discount them if they don't agree with your own?
    - Consider how they might improve your current perception?
    - Involve others in discussing how different perceptions can enhance your outcomes?
3. Do you proactively solicit others perceptions?
4. Do you share your perceptions with others?

Your Rudder

It takes a lot of skill and experience, along with the right equipment, to safely sail a ship across the seas. Primary among that equipment is the rudder. It determines the vessel's direction and gives the sailor a way to steer the ship and avoid dangers. What would happen to a ship if it were rudderless? It would travel aimlessly, pushed by whatever currents and winds it came across.

Consider your values, the ethics, standards and morals in which you believe. What you value determines how you deal with the world. Values help you decide what is right or wrong, good or bad. Values are like a ship's rudder; they determine the direction you take.

Compromise your values and you become like a rudderless ship. Without your values, you could lose the respect and trust of the people who sail with you. You will also sacrifice your own self-respect and personal integrity.

As a manager, you manage things and as a leader, you lead people. Successful leadership is based on the degree of trust you have established with your people. If they see consistency between your values and your actions, they will trust you to sail their ship. So, don't forget your rudder. There are already too many rudderless ships afloat.

Application Questions

1. What is the relationship between your values and your actions? Are you consistent?
2. What are some reactions you might see or hear from a team led by someone who says one thing yet does another?
3. Why are personal values so critical in any endeavor?
4. How does the principle of values impact a team?
5. What can you do to ensure your values are visible and believable?

Who, Me?

Former President Harry Truman used the saying, "The buck stops here", to explain how he felt about accepting the responsibilities of his office. Unfortunately, some managers seem to have forgotten that responsibility and accountability are inherent in the job.

Managers who do not take personal responsibility for the results of their business unit, those who "pass the buck", weaken their company's future and their own. At all levels within a company, whether you are dealing with strategies or tactics it makes no difference. When you accepted the role of manager you became responsible and accountable for the results of your unit. If you won't stand up for the results of your team who should? Let's be very clear here, you are accountable.

If not you, who?

Application Questions

1. What are you specifically responsible and accountable for?
2. How was this communicated to you?
3. How have you communicated with each of your team, what they are responsible and accountable for respectively?
4. What consequences have you set in place to ensure your team acts in a responsible and accountable manner?
5. How do you coach your team on this?
6. How do you assign levels of authority for your team members to carry out their tasks?
7. What could you do to improve people taking responsibility for their actions and results?
8. How could you role model this?

Behavior is Believable

The walls of the processing department displayed a series of framed corporate vision statements; "Customer Service is our business", "We exist to serve our customers", "We are the Customer Care Company!" At the back of the long, rectangular room was the manager's office. A glass wall separated the manager's office from the rest of the department.

Because customer service was one of the critical strategies for the company's success, they periodically surveyed and rated each department based on feedback from internal and external customers. The processing department's scores were dismal and declining.

Out of frustration, Ralph, the processing manager had called in help. He had asked the service director to observe his staff to find the cause of the problem.

After observing the department for several weeks, the service director met with Ralph to report his findings. He said, "Well, I did see that sometimes phones were left to ring. Some people who had finished their work were sitting around and not offering to help anyone else. Your people seemed indifferent about their work and each other."

Ralph broke in, "Before you tell me how you are going to solve this, I just want to say that if I had the chance, I'd fire half of them and get me some better people, but since I can't, I have to work with what I have. So what's your solution?"

The service director left his chair and, walking over to the glass wall, turned to face Ralph. "First, there is something else I noticed. Whenever you walk through the department, whether arriving in the morning, passing through to a meeting or leaving at the end of the day, you never say one word of greeting, acknowledgement, or even a sign of recognition to your team. It is as if they are invisible to you. In the service meeting I attended you read the service standards and berated everyone about their need to shape up and improve the department's scores."

"I think I have found the source of the problem and it is you. Service slogans, speeches, plaques on the wall, all the platitudes you can say are never as powerful as what you do. Your team has looked at your behavior and taken their cue as to what to do from it. Ralph, you had better start leading by example because your actions belie your words."

Application Questions
1. Why is the saying, 'Don't do what I do, do what I tell you to do', a poor leadership and management strategy?
2. What are some of the behaviors you do that you want others on your team to do?
3. What behaviors could you do that would improve individual performance in your team?
4. Why is being a role model an important function for a manager?
5. What is one behavior that if it were improved, would make the most difference in the perception of your team as being good role models for other teams?

Change Leaders Needed

Whether you want to or not, you need to continually reinvent your business in order to stay in business. Realizing this, senior management is quick to talk about the 'need for change', but very often they are disappointed in the results of their change initiatives. Why is this?

One of the key reasons is because championing change does not often appear in the job description of most managers, including the CEO's. Managers often aren't encouraged to 'think outside the box' and when they do, they frequently are not rewarded for their efforts. The focus is typically on quarterly results, and not as much on what they can do at their level to improve performance.

So if you want to create an organization that is continually engaged in perfecting the 'customer experience' through any number of change initiatives, you have to start by making every manager at every level an advocate for change, a Change Agent. How do you do this?

Start by asking yourself if your managers know that you expect them to embrace change, support it, and even lead it. Is this an expectation of their jobs?

Then, ask yourself if you demonstrate—by your actions— the way a Change Agent should behave, because, if you don't, it is highly probable that they won't. We tend to look at what our leader says and does as indicators of what we should say and do.

How do managers demonstrate their affinity for change? Here are a few examples to consider.

They look at their business from the customer's point of view. They make it a point to 'shop' their business. They let everyone know they are going to do this to see what it's like to be a customer of the organization. They call the call center and ask for information. They call different departments to see how the phone is answered. They visit offices and stores to see how customers are treated. This is the best way they can know what it is their customers experience. If they don't know that, how can they continually improve it, even reinvent it?

Being curious and shopping gives you the opportunity to recognize outstanding performance and reward it. Give specific on-the-spot verbal recognition such as, "I am pleased to see you have set up weekly coaching on our change initiative with your people. I'd like you to share how you do this with the rest of the managers." Write personal notes commenting on what the manager has done that is in keeping with your expectations. Give managers who demonstrate their support of the change rewards and recognition, they are powerful motivators.

Shopping also points out where improvements are needed. Be quick to point these out and clarify what it is you want to improve and follow up to see that it is done. Without follow up, managers often will not make the improvement a priority.

Curiosity prevents you from relying on customer surveys to tell you what your customers want. Someone once asked Henry Ford why he hadn't asked people what they wanted in transportation when he was designing his first automobile. He said because they would have said, "faster horses". So don't expect customers to tell you. They don't know what they don't know.

These managers encourage ideas from outside. They are always looking for best practices and they expect their people to try things out. That means they encourage continual 'tinkering' with the processes, procedures, protocols of the business. And, as a part of this experimenting and exploring, they coach their people on how to take prudent risks so that decisions can be made in the field with confidence.

Finally, they continually talk up the value of change. They support those who are trying to make the change work and they coach those who are not.

Make being an advocate for change a part of every manager's job description including your own.

Application Questions

1. What changes are being made in your business now?
2. What changes are being planned?
3. Why are these changes important to your business?
4. Who (employees, departments, divisions) is or will be effected by current and future changes?
5. What specifically do you expect managers to do to lead and support changes?
6. How have the managers of the impacted areas been prepared to lead and support these changes?
7. How sure are you that they can do this?
8. What is your involvement in the changes now and in the future?
9. What actions do you need to take to improve the effectiveness of the changes you are currently making or planning to make in the future?

Change Isn't Your Problem

We change when we want to. We change boyfriends and girlfriends, husbands and wives, cars, houses, towns and jobs. We even change the color of our hair, don't we? When we get sufficiently dissatisfied with the status quo we make a change, and not always for the better, but we do change. The thing is we make changes when they are under our own control, when we are part of the decision to change.

But, sometimes we get change forced upon us and we aren't part of the decision. We aren't in control. This is the problem that managers often face. It is loss of control that brings out our defenses. At work, most of us can accept changes in procedures, protocols, and processes if they are small or introduced incrementally, so we can absorb them, over time. But, when we get blasted by a dramatic change in how we operate and we're expected to accommodate to it quickly, our resistance comes into play and the change often isn't implemented well.

A top European financial company's executive management team embarked on a three-pronged initiative involving changes in their technology, their processing procedures and their sales approach. It all made perfect sense to them. As they saw it, time was of the essence. They had to make these changes because competition was heating up and if they didn't do something quickly, they would lose market share.

The entire initiative was introduced in a manager's meeting after which the managers were to go back and explain to their people the reason for this major initiative. As all three changes impacted the sales force, these employees found all aspects of their jobs were changing weekly as the three projects rolled out.

For a change to get seated as an accepted business habit, it has to be practiced until it can be done almost automatically. That is the point where both confidence and competence merge. Unfortunately, in most businesses there is never enough time for this to happen. It's up to the manager to take control of the rate and speed of change for the team. It's up to the manager to prioritize training toward the critical aspects of the change and to support employees through the training process.

If you want to speed up acceptance of a major change, make sure your managers are well prepared to introduce it properly. Allow them to discuss what they think their employees will be concerned about and help them to prepare what they will say to introduce the change. In other words equip your managers to support the change and help lead the process.

Application Questions

1. How do you introduce change(s) to your team? What else could you do?
2. What do you do to get them receptive to the change(s)? What more could you do?
3. How do you follow up to ensure your people are implementing the change(s)? What else could you do?
4. What do you do to support those who are trying to make the change(s)? What more could you do?
5. What do you do to help those having difficulty making the change(s)? What else could you do?

Managing Change Means Changing How You Manage

Ever hear that old phrase, "If you do what you've always done, you'll get what you've always got"? That certainly applies when you are responsible for managing changes to the way your people work. A 22 billion dollar commercial bank instituted the use of customer profiling and an integrated computer database. These two changes impacted the sales force. What did they do to manage such changes?

First, they changed job descriptions so that they reflected what the jobs now needed in terms of experience, knowledge and skills. Then they changed the training plans for their people to include new training requirements. In addition, they revised performance evaluations to include manager observations of employee ability to use the new computer system as well as their competence with the new sales approach. The last item meant changing what managers looked for and the way they coached for improvement.

So when a change is introduced in your business understand that there really are two changes going on. One is the change itself and the other is the change you must make in how you manage that change with your team.

Application Questions
1. Why should you change how you manage when changes are introduced to your business units' business operations and methods?
2. How do you set expectations for a change to be successful?
3. How should your job description reflect those changes?
4. If your position changes, should that mean that your boss's job should also change? In what way?

Tuning Up

I once had a neighbor who devoted his free time to tinkering with his Chevy. I asked him why he spent so much time working on the car that seemed to be in mint condition. He said he had two reasons. The first was to prevent a possible problem from happening. The second was because he enjoyed seeing if he could make the ride even smoother, the engine more efficient.

Managers could adopt this attitude toward their work. Lift the 'hood' on your policies, procedures and methods and check out how they're working for your customers. Do any need to be replaced or updated to prevent a future breakdown? Does your staff believe that forms and procedures could be 'rewired' to make them more efficient?

Consider this: If you were going to sell your part of the business, how would it stack up against similar departments on the sales lot?

Tuning up helps prevent breakdowns and can prevent making your operation obsolete. Always remember, your business can choose to change or be forced to accept changes forced upon it. Go on tinker away.

Application Questions

1. What are the systems, procedures, processes my team is responsible for?
2. How do we measure the effectiveness of the teams' output?
3. What actions do we routinely take to review them?
4. How often do we evaluate the systems, procedures and processes?
5. What kinds of complaints do we receive about these? Are these increasing or decreasing?
6. What expectations have I set with my team for working to continuously improve?
7. How do I show support for improvement suggestions from the team?
8. What could I do to be more proactive when it comes to continuous improvement?

Ego Box

Managers can have a passion for their business, but the running of a business should be dispassionate.

Managers need a small box in their top desk drawer for their egos. When they come to work, they should open the box and tuck their emotional ego inside. Then, when the boss or a client challenges them or a peer questions their idea or an employee causes a problem, they can focus on the situation without allowing emotions to drive their reactions.

Here is a case in point. The owner of a Midwestern manufacturing firm had an ego the size of Cleveland, Ohio. When someone brought up an idea for a business strategy, he ridiculed it. When someone recommended changes in their production methods, he would try to draw other employees in to side with him against the change. More time was spent on placating and nursing his ego than on making decisions that would move the company forward.

One sure way to lower your perceived effectiveness is to engage your ego in place of your brain.

Application Questions

1. How do you know when you are letting your ego get in the way of good judgment?
2. What can letting emotions control your actions end up costing you?
3. What situations are most likely to cause your ego to become involved?
4. What can you do to avoid involving your ego in these situations?
5. Does any of your team have a problem with their ego?
6. How can you use yourself as an example for your team?

Arrogance of Command

Be careful not to believe too much in your own press. It's a great feeling to be in a very successful business, or to have a string of successful sales or projects. If your success streak lasts long enough, it's easy to forget what it took to get there and who helped along the way. If you become blinded by your record of results, you are setting yourself up for a dangerous fall. There will be those who will enjoy watching you pass by on your way down.

How does someone act arrogant? It could be the manager who is 'too busy' to talk with his people or doesn't see the need to keep them informed or takes credit for their contributions. It might be the manager who only talks to 'important' customers while ignoring all others.

Fifteen years of stair-step earnings increases made the CEO of a regional bank believe he was invincible. He began to make riskier credit decisions in order to continue his 10% per year growth in earnings. He rode rough-shod over his board of directors and his key managers, because, after all he was a winner according to his track record. Then the economy began to falter and some of his riskier credit decisions went bad. It wasn't long before he was replaced.

As long as you are winning, payback for this flaw might not come due. But, if you ever have problems, and you will, payback will be like a loan that has gone bad, due on demand. You will pay.

Application Questions
1. If you have a strong track record, what are some of the things you do to keep a level head?
2. How do you treat people who are helping you succeed?
3. What are some of the things you have seen others do that have had a negative impact on their reputation and possibly career?
4. What do you need to do to avoid this happening to you?

The Palace Guards

Get to know the guards. Every business has them. These are managers who are entrusted to send communications up and down the management mountain. They ensure that the leaders are fully informed on daily happenings in the business. They convey strategies down the mountain to be acted upon. When they are working in the best interests of the business they perform a valuable and necessary function.

But, sometimes the guards 'over-inflate' their importance and lose sight of their mission. They begin to decide what the leader needs to hear and what the organization needs to know. They start acting in the leader's place. When this happens, the business is headed for trouble.

Management that selects palace guards and doesn't periodically check the validity of what they say and do should not be surprised when there is management by 'innuendo' and more time is spent on politics and who is aligned with whom than on the business of business. Morale begins a slow decline that picks up speed as fear and uncertainty fuel the coffee breaks. The surest sign that there is a major landslide coming on the mountain is that overall results suffer and no one can figure out why!

Application Questions
1. How do communications flow in your business? Consider these factors:
   - Frequency of information from the top down and the bottom up
   - clarity of information
   - accuracy of information
   - follow up to verify messages have been passed on
   - lack of bottlenecks
   - amount of misinformation given by Palace Guards

2. What kinds of information do you share with your team? Does it include:
   - company vision, mission and values
   - yearly goals, strategies and tactics for achieving the goals of the company
   - your units' vision, goals, strategies and tactics
   - responses to negative information
   - responses to positive information
   - frequent formal and informal communications

The Balancing Act

Sometimes, balancing all the parts of your life is like trying to ride a bicycle across a tightrope while juggling lighted batons. For starters, you have your family, and then there are your friends and neighbors, the people you work with and of course, your boss.

Oh, and let's not forget your other obligations. Perhaps there are church activities, the course you're trying to take at the local college, the PTA, and the health club you paid for but rarely visit. And, while you pause to catch your breath think about those other things you like to do, you know hobbies, sports, social stuff.

The problem is time. You have 168 hours a week to spend. Spend too much on work and your family and friends suffer. You could try to 'borrow' some time by dropping the college course or the health club. You could give up your hobby so you have more time for the family.

Face it. The stress of balancing all the demands on your time leads to anxiety over things not getting done and guilt over not 'being there' when you feel you should. So, what are your priorities? It's been said that the essence of life is in the journey, not the destination. Make *appointments* with yourself, your family and friends. Measure your success in terms of your whole life, not just your job.

Application Questions

1. Where are you currently spending your time? Make a list of these areas.

2. Thinking in terms of a week of time, 168 hours, write down the amount of time you currently spend with each area on the list. For example, if you spend ten hours a day working for five days of the week, write down 50 hours.

3. Are there any areas that aren't getting enough of your time? Put a check by those.

4. Are there some areas where you are spending too much time? Put an X by those.

5. Can you 'borrow' time from one area to spend on another?

6. If your time is unbalanced, is this a temporary or permanent situation?

7. What changes can you make if:
   - your workload is robbing you of time
   - you are missing family events
   - you have no personal time

The Power of Why

Before you present your plan for increasing sales, reducing costs, buying new equipment, or adding to staff, present it to yourself out loud. For each major point you want to make, ask yourself the 'why' question. Ask yourself, why this step? Why not something else? Ask yourself, why include these people and why not others? Ask, why now and why not some other time? Finally, ask why will this help the company and why not something else? Anticipate all the questions you might be asked and prepare your answers to them.

The only true way you know if you are prepared to sell your plan is when you can articulate it aloud. If you can't explain it clearly and convincingly to yourself, why should anyone else believe it?

Application Questions
1. Rehearsing aloud may help prevent you from making what kinds of mistakes?
2. How does asking 'why questions' increase your self-confidence and your presentation?
3. Reflect on some of your presentations:
   - For any in which you did not rehearse, would that practice have improved them?
   - For any in which you did not apply 'why questions', would this practice have made a difference?
4. How could you involve your team in improving their presentations?

What If

Pilots have to have flight plans. These plans show where they are going, where they intend to land. But every pilot also has alternate landing fields along the way where they can land if they have to. They keep these in mind in case they have a 'what if' occur. A 'what if' is a contingency that makes it impossible for the plane to reach its intended destination.

When managers develop their business plans, they would do well to consider alternate actions they can take that will get them to their overall objective whether that is profitability, efficiency, growth or even survival. Ask the question; 'what if' to surface possible contingencies that could occur and determine what alternatives you might take that could still get you to your overall objective.

If you are tracking progress toward your plan objective on a routine basis, you'll be able to switch actions or tactics if you need to and not have the plan end in disaster.

The head of retail for a 45 billion dollar consumer bank had a plan for increasing deposit growth through an advertising campaign aimed at bringing in new customers. But, when the marketing department couldn't come up with what the bank wanted for print, radio and television, the retail head reallocated the money to the branch managers in the form of employee bonus money. He told the managers that since there would be no advertising or campaign materials, it was up to each branch to heighten their deposit referral and sales goals. Those exceeding their goals would receive bonus money equal to the percentage of the increase over their goals. This approach was very successful and got the retail area to their overall deposit growth goal.

Application Questions
1. What kind of contingencies can affect your plan or processes?
2. Why is it not a good idea to modify your goals instead of finding alternatives to achieving them?
3. For each goal you have for this year, what else, other than what you have in the plan, might you do if a 'what if' occurs?

Three Elements That Make a Plan Succeed

For plans to succeed they need to answer three questions. First, what is the plan's goal, second, what measurement of that goal will indicate success and third, when does it need to be reached. Without numbers two and three the plan is not a plan. Oh, you can add all kinds of specifics and qualifiers into the plan, but the essence of the plan is found in the answers to these three questions.

For example, let's say in your business you want to increase the number of first-time buyers. That in and of itself isn't a plan. That's the first part of the three-part plan. If instead you say you want to increase your number of first-time buyers by 10% by the end of second quarter you have a plan. You can build specific actions and measures to chart your progress against this plan.

The question most often ignored is the one of time. It's not difficult to say increase sales by 10%. By adding a time deadline you increase urgency and enhance the chances that actions will be taken to realize the plan.

A manager explained the importance of time to a plan this way. "Without adding the element of time you are engaging in prayerful management. You might as well clasp your hands together, look up to the heavens and pray, 'I hope they do it, I hope they do it'."

Application Questions

1. Whether you make a plan for achieving your business goals or plan a project, do you always ensure you have covered the three bases of specifically what you want to do, how much of it you need to do and when it needs to be done?

2. How much difference does having all three bases covered have on your success?

3. How can having all three bases included in a plan impact employee motivation?

4. Think about an experience you have had in planning that was not as successful as you hoped. What could you have done differently? Consider:
    - Was the goal or objective specific enough?
    - Was the goal attainable with reasonable effort?
    - Did you have a simple way to measure it?
    - Was the timeframe clear and doable?
    - Did you follow up consistently on actions taken and give feedback and coach?

When Is a Nice-To-Do a Must-Do?

There are basically two ways a business ensures its future. It increases profitable revenues and it decreases expenses. That's it. Strategic plans are built around the 'must-dos', not the 'nice-to-dos'.

Oh sure, when times are really good some of the nice-to-dos will work their way into the plan. But at the first sign of a downturn, watch how quickly they are dropped. In one company, the economic barometer was the professionally cared-for- plants on every floor; whenever management eliminated 'the plants', it signaled bad times.

Senior management hopes that their managers understand that their part of the yearly plan should answer this simple question; "Will what your plan do to make us money or save us money"? If it doesn't relate to one or the other or both in a measurable way, it may well be eliminated.

The challenge is finding a way for the nice-to-do to qualify as a must-do. Office plants may not make it over the long haul, but renovating an office so customers have more attractive surroundings and more privacy in which to conduct their business can measurably increase customer satisfaction, leading to more sales.

Another classic example is internal training programs. Unless their objectives have a direct correlation to making money or saving money they are often cut when times are tight. But, if as a result of training, they are able to see an increase in sales or a decrease in processing time because of a lower error rate then training may be considered a 'must-do'. Often what appears on the surface to be a 'nice-to-do' can be turned into a 'must-do' by showing its return on investment, its R.O.I.

Application Questions
1. Have you provided benefit statements for each major goal or objective in your plan?
2. Are these worded so that it is clear how they will make your company money or save them money?
3. In addition, have you described the extent of revenue gain or cost savings you are projecting?
4. Have you specified any tactics or actions you will take to achieve this and by when?
5. Do you follow this approach for projects as well?

Aligning Objectives

One of the factors that determine an organization's success is how well each manager's business unit objectives support the objectives of the other managers as well as the overriding plan for the business. That's why senior executives need to become adept at strategic and tactical planning. They need to make sure all plans mesh, enabling the company to achieve its strategic goals.

Here is an example of what happens when objectives have been left to work in opposition to each other. A number of years ago, I worked with a company that wanted to find out why their sales figures were lower than planned. The company had spent millions to put in a computerized database which enabled every sales person to record all sales related activities, proposals, meetings, even calls with prospects. Their expectation was that the system, combined with the good products they had would lead to higher sales. So far, this wasn't the case.

The head of sales told me that they had a lot of business in their pipeline but it wasn't showing up as they had to queue up to input data because they had two computers for the 12 sales people in the department. When I asked why he hadn't gotten more computers, he told me, "The guy in charge of purchasing won't approve my request."

I was curious why purchasing wouldn't approve a request for such obviously needed equipment, so I met with the purchasing manager and he explained it this way. "My primary objective for this year is to reduce costs in equipment and materials. Computers are one place I can cut expenses. Next year I will include the sales request in my budget."

So sales would languish and they would lose business because the sales staff was sharing two computers and couldn't access their sales database in a timely manner. The strategic objective of the company—sales growth—was going to be impacted. Purchasing would achieve its objective of reducing equipment costs, but at an expense to the company!

Make sure all primary objectives support the overall goals of the company by encouraging cooperation among business units. In fact, make that an objective in every plan. Whenever you hear management talk about the 'silos' in their business, you can be sure they aren't encouraging cooperation and everyone is focused on doing their own thing.

Application Questions

1. Have you ever been in a situation where a manager achieved their goals at the expense of another manager? What were the repercussions?
2. Besides referring business to other business units, what else could be done to assist other managers in the completion of their objectives?
3. How is aligning objectives an example of true teamwork?
4. What happens to teamwork within the company when employees see unit leaders concentrating on only their own objectives?
5. What do you need to do to ensure you are cooperating with others to align objectives? Consider:
   • What other business units you interface with, those you impact and those that are impacted by you.
   • What are examples of how you could help each other?
   • What changes could you make?
   • How could you initiate this?

Sometimes Right is Wrong

A project manager found her project stalled because her boss, the head of marketing, hadn't provided the marketing data as requested. At the next project meeting, with all the marketing managers in attendance, she brought this fact to everyone's attention, and was never heard from again.

You may be entirely right in your evaluation of the situation, but this is one time when you need to bring it up respectfully, in private. Never make your boss look bad in front of others.

Application Questions

1. How can you work with a boss/senior manager to prevent such a 'political-management' problem from happening?
   - When a project/initiative is assigned?
   - Using one-on-one meetings?
   - During team meetings?
   - Using written communications such as email, memos, reports

Consider the Source

Sincere compliments have no strings attached. When you receive one, enjoy it; bask in it, save it up for your next tough day. However, not all compliments are sincere. Sometimes a compliment is made because the person giving it wants something in return. It might be your support for a project they are working on or it might be to back them on a recommendation they are making for a change in the company. If you were going to give that support anyway, you have no problem. Just make sure you are not supporting others because of the 'kind words' they have said about you.

Some who are adept at company politics use compliments and innuendos to further their position. Innuendos are spread to others to create doubt about someone's abilities or value to the company. If you are getting negative press you can either ignore it or confront the individual.

In both cases, before you react, consider the source. Have you seen or heard this person use compliments or innuendos to manipulate others before? If so, then don't put much faith or weight in what has been said because probably no one else will.

Application Questions
1. How do you know if a compliment is sincere?
2. How do you know if a compliment has strings attached?
3. How can you acknowledge the compliment without committing yourself to anything?
4. If you know you are working with a manipulator, why is acknowledging their compliment a safe thing to do?
5. If you don't acknowledge it, could they possibly begin a campaign of innuendos?

Be a Business Owner

How many managers tolerate mediocre or poor performance? Enough to cost companies millions, even billions of dollars in lost sales and poor service. Why is this so?

Not too long ago, the manager in a branch office of a major American bank was reviewing the sales performance of his staff with his division manager. The division manager noticed that of the five sales employees, one had only sold on average, one product per week for the past three months! He asked the branch manager what he was doing about this employee. The branch manager said, "Oh, you know she's been here for years, all the customers know her. She gives good service; sales just aren't her strong suit."

The division manager replied, "Since she's not meeting her sales goals, that means the others are supposed to make up for her, and they aren't doing that. All of which means you will once again fail to meet your goals for this quarter."

He went on, "What would happen if you owned this branch and you were not making a profit but still had to pay the salary and benefits of your staff out of your own pocket"?

The branch manager thought for a minute and then said, "Well, I would have to let her go. I couldn't afford to keep her."

Act like you own your part of the business. It will make a meaningful difference in how you manage it.

Application Questions
1. With the exception of new employees, do you have any employees whose productivity is below acceptable levels?
2. What actions have you taken to help them improve their results?
    - Do they know what is expected of them? How do you know this?
    - Have they demonstrated they know how to?
    - Have they been coached by you or others?
    - What consequences have you set?
3. How do you follow up to observe their performance on the job?
4. How would acting like a business owner change the way you manage?

There Is No Freedom without Discipline

A number of years before I became a business consultant, I taught junior and senior high school in California and Texas. This was at the time of Flower Power, the Black Panthers, the Vietnam War and a host of other seismic shifts in American culture. What was happening in society at large was replicated to differing degrees in the schools.

I taught junior high in San Diego in the early sixties. The school was racially divided into Asian, Black, Hispanic and white students. Because of the unrest in the community, many of the students were unruly and kept testing their limits. In one semester, a teacher was badly beaten because he had suspended two boys for fighting. Another teacher was accosted with a switchblade knife in her classroom. A seventh grade girl gave birth in the bathroom, and left the baby on the floor.

In Texas, I taught in a junior high where most of the students were latchkey children living in nearby apartments. Many times they would go to their homes for lunch and return high on drugs. They had what they called 'pill parties' in which they dumped all the pills they could find into a bowl and each grabbed a handful to wash down with Cokes. When they came back to the school they were incapable of learning anything. Final week was a nightmare with several students in one of my classes passing out and needing medical attention. And to top it off, one boy was injured when someone threw a pipe bomb into the boys' bathroom. School officials were not much help in the Texas school. The principal locked himself in his office.

In the sixties and early seventies schools were involved in the great permissive experiment. The theory was, let children be involved in running their schools, let them express themselves. Let them 'find' themselves.

Why bring this up in a book about leadership and management? Because when there is no discipline or structure nor any accountability for actions, society breaks down. It's true in the schools, it's true in society and it's true in business. People need to know the rules and they need to know they will be accountable for what they do.

Think about your town, what would happen if overnight all the stop lights and road signs were removed. What would the morning commute be like?

Application Questions
1. If structure refers to how you are organized, how you communicate, your policies and procedures and discipline refers to accountabilities and consequences, what kind of structure and discipline exists in your company?
2. If you could, what changes to the structure and sets of disciplines would you make to improve effectiveness and efficiencies?
3. What do you have in place with your own team?
4. Could this be improved? How?

Go On, Have a Sense of Humor

For some people, moving into the upper realm of management means distancing themselves from the other employees and adopting a serious demeanor. These people seem to have lost the ability to laugh at situations and worst of all, themselves.

The sales departments for a large company decided to have a western barbecue on a ranch for their annual sales conference. Everyone came in cowboy attire, except for the head of sales. He sat at a table dressed in expensive slacks and a sports coat, clearly sending a message that he wasn't part of the fun.

Another example that was talked about for weeks happened during a fire drill in the headquarters of a regional corporation. Seems a large number of the employees had evacuated to their parking lot immediately adjacent to the building. Someone on an upper floor threw down two of the stuffed corporate mascot dolls, yelling, "Save my babies, save my babies!" Everyone laughed except for one very senior executive, who glared up at the offender and stalked off.

People like to feel their boss is human, too. Showing a sense of humor does not diminish you, it creates stronger bonds with those who want to follow you.

Application Questions
1. What do you do to create a comfort zone between yourself and others?
2. What is the danger of getting too close to your team members or other managers?
3. Do you create better relationships through such actions as laughing at your own mistakes, self-disclosing safe personal information, sharing humorous stories? What else could you do?

Run With What You Brung

The quickest way to shoot yourself in the foot is to tell senior management that you can't take on a new challenge unless you have more staff or more equipment or more money. The minute you say this you have labeled yourself as just one of the many mediocre managers within your company. Why? Because you have said you are not up to the challenge, you are not creative or willing to be innovative to get the job done. Instead, put together a plan for what you can do using the resources at your disposal and present it to your management. What they want is that kind of can-do attitude.

A manager once explained it to me this way. "It's like this; management says to you, "Do you see that pit of lions down there? Well, we want you to put them back in their cages. Now we have a whip and a chair, but we aren't going to give them to you. So you go down into the pit and you fight those lions. Finally, you crawl out of the pit, clothes torn, body scratched and bloody and you say. 'Look, I got the lions back into their cages.' Management says that's good. Here's your whip and your chair, but they aren't going to help you with that fire breathing dragon. Now, we need you to put him back in his cave. We have a fire extinguisher and an asbestos suit, but we aren't going to give them to you . . . yet."

Application Questions
1. How have you reacted to these types of challenges in the past?
2. What made you successful or unsuccessful?
3. Why does management set up these challenges? Are they testing you?
4. What will you do the next time you are given a challenge?
5. Do you set up challenges for members of your team?
6. Do you need to?

Keep your Promises

One of the most highly valued traits you can have is keeping your word. You say, "I'll call you back this afternoon", and you do! You tell someone, "You'll get that proposal by 3:00 tomorrow", and they do! You respond to an email saying, "I will email you the research numbers before the end of the day", and they get them before 5:00!

Why is keeping your word so important? Because when you keep your word you build trust with the other person. Trust is built upon predictability and being predictable means you do what you say.

A client located in London was considering hiring someone for an important management spot. The candidate had impressed everyone and his credentials fit the needs of the position. In fact, they were in the process of putting together the offer letter when one of the references they had been trying to reach called them back. He verified all the experiences the candidate had listed and then he added this comment. "The only thing that annoyed me when I worked with Lloyd was that he seemed indifferent to following up on calls, even meetings sometimes. He always had an excuse but it was annoying."

You are in a people business. When people trust you, they will follow you. So be known for your predictability by keeping your word.

Application Questions
1. Do you keep your word?
2. If something prevents you from doing so, what do you do to still keep others' trust?
3. How do you handle the situation when a team member or colleague fails to keep their word?
4. What else can you do to improve the perception of your team as trustworthy?
5. How should you communicate the value of trust to your team?

The Good News and the Bad News about Success

I was seated next to a good-looking Marine in his full dress uniform on a flight from Washington D.C. to Los Angeles. He could have just stepped off a recruiting poster, he looked so good. I complimented him on his uniform and asked if he had been in Washington for anything special.

He said, "Oh, yes, ma'am. I won this year's Recruiter of the Year Award for exceeding my quota of new recruits. I just attended a luncheon to receive my award."

"Congratulations," I said. "You must be very proud."

"Well, yes, I am," he replied, "but I am kind of worried about next year."

"Why is that?" I asked.

He gave a little laugh and then said, "The bad news about winning is they up your quota for next year."

Often in business the same is true. It is called, rising expectations. If you meet your goal, management expects you can do it and more the next time.

Application Questions
1. Can 'rising expectations' be demotivating?
2. What can you do to reduce or even prevent demotivation from happening?
3. Which of these actions have been helpful to you in motivating yourself and your team to meet higher goals?
   - Chunk the overall goal down into smaller pieces with shorter time focuses
   - Assign parts of the goal to each team member based on their knowledge, experience and skills
   - Celebrate, reward and recognize when individual goals are achieved
   - Coach to improve skills and knowledge
   - Collaborate with others to get ideas to improve your own capabilities
4. What might you do now, that you weren't doing before?

Row Your Boat

A business unit or department is like a life boat. You might not have chosen the people in your boat, and they certainly didn't choose each other. Nevertheless, you are in the boat together. Your success as the leader requires you to get everyone to row together. No one can rest at the oars while others row. No one can hoard resources while others do without. Your job is to organize the people and coordinate their efforts. Then, if there is a sea change in the company or the economy, your life boat can make it through to safety.

Everyone in the boat needs to know the goal, where you are rowing to. Everyone needs to know how they can contribute and help each other so their boat stays afloat. And, everyone needs to know their progress. From time to time, you need to pull up on the oars, coast a bit and celebrate the distance you have come.

Oh, and be sure to take your turn at the oars. After all, you're in the boat, too.

Application Questions

1. Of the following actions, which are your responsibilities as captain of the boat?

- Watching your rowers
- Helping anyone who is having trouble rowing
- Checking progress again your map of the goal
- Visiting other boats to talk with other captains
- Passing out supplies
- Supervising the allocation of supplies
- Encouraging the crew

2. Of these actions, which ones are you doing consistently (daily/weekly)?

3. What else could you do that would improve your life in your boat?

The Spinning Plates

There's an old variety act in which a juggler spins china plates on top of bamboo poles to the music of "Flight of the Bumble Bee". As the music increases in tempo, the juggler runs back and forth re-spinning those plates that are beginning to wobble and adding more poles and plates. This continues until he can no longer support all the spinning plates and they begin to fall and break. The act is timed so that as the plates start crashing, the music ends. Of course, the audience enjoys the juggler's frantic efforts, knowing that he can't keep up the momentum.

While this may be an entertaining act, it isn't so funny when managers behave like that juggler, taking on more and more tasks and projects without handing off any of the previous tasks to others on the team. Of course, handing off projects takes some upfront time to train and coach people so the tasks can be delegated to them. But unless managers do this, sooner or later, two things will happen. One, some of the 'plates' will fall, meaning a project or a plan will not be successful, and two, this will cause their bosses to lose confidence in their abilities proving once again the old Peter Principle, "Managers rise to the level of their incompetence" .

Application Questions

1. Are you currently doing anything to prepare others so you can delegate some of your tasks to them?
2. What tasks can't you delegate?
3. What tasks can you delegate?
4. What are some of the actions you can take to prepare others to accept new tasks?

Never Stop Dating

Ever watch couples in a restaurant? Over at the table by the window sits a young couple. She's been telling her date about something, she's excited about. She's gesturing with her hands and smiling as she speaks. The young man is leaning forward, one elbow on the table, his hand cupping his chin. He is staring intently, smiling and nodding from time to time.

At the table next to you is a middle-aged married couple. They sit in silence, looking around the room, not at each other. Their dinner arrives. Both begin to eat. You overhear the husband say, "How's your meal?"

The difference between these two couples illustrates a basic communications problem. You build receptivity with others by showing you are interested in what they say, therefore you are interested in them. Affirmation is absolutely essential to all of us because it is central to our self-esteem.

Be like the young couple.

Application Questions

1. What are some of the things you do to show you are interested in what someone has to say?

2. What are some of the things you have observed others doing to show they are not interested in a conversation?

3. On this list, what one thing, that you are not doing now, could you do to make you communicate more effectively?

    - keep eye contact
    - face the person
    - have a relaxed stance or posture
    - nod or smile
    - make encouraging sounds ("oh?")
    - don't interrupt or take control of the conversation unless they ask you to
    - empathize
    - self-disclose

Snowbound

Ever lived where it snows? If so, does this sound familiar? It is after 5:00 p.m. on a dark winter's day and you are anxious to get home. You watched snow falling all afternoon and now you tramp through half a foot or so of the damp stuff to your car. You scrap the windshield and back window clear and warm up the motor.

All around you, tires whine on the snow as cars pull out of the lot. Now you shift into reverse and press the gas. Your tires spin uselessly in the deep snow. You shift forward and again, the tires spin. Ah ha! You think, "I know what to do. I'll give it more gas and rock the car loose!" Back and forth you rock. Forward, reverse, forward; reverse, until you admit you are stuck. Doing more of the same thing didn't work.

You can get just as stuck when you are trying to communicate. You are in a meeting with someone whose support you need. You can see you are losing their interest and attention. Instead of backing off, in desperation you add more points, talk more urgently, try harder to convince.

When you realize you are getting stuck, ease off. Ask questions and listen. You may find the right way to move forward.

Application Questions
1. How can you tell when you have lost someone's interest and attention?
2. What do you do in this case?
3. When should you prepare some questions that can be used to get your conversation back on track? Before you meet or when you are stuck?
4. Is there ever a time when you should just stop and ask to reschedule? Why?
5. Is it ever the fault of the other person, or is it always your responsibility to keep the person interested?

Focus, Focus

Charles Emerson Winchester III, a surgeon on the old television program, 'M*A*S*H', was criticized by his colleagues for taking too long when operating.

He responded rather pompously, "I do one thing, I do it incredibly well and then I move on."

That may not have been the best approach during combat surgery, but it does make a valid point. The ability to focus on what you are doing enables you to do your best work.

Have you ever been at your desk trying to complete a report or a proposal and you hear someone on your staff discussing a problem with a customer? You can hear that the call isn't going well. You're half listening to what is going on as you re-read what you have just written. You shuffle through your papers looking for some projections, but the distraction continues. When you finally find the numbers, the point you wanted to make with them eludes you. You glance at the clock and feel your frustration level rise.

There will always be distractions and interruptions. When they start to get to you, ask yourself, "What should be my focus?" If you think multitasking will reduce your problems, think again. You may have several projects, meetings and calls that need to be done, the secret to your success is to prioritize based on importance and time and then: Do one thing at a time, do it well. And then move on.

Application Questions
1. What do you do to organize your work to accomplish the most you can?
2. How often do you find you have to reorganize because of new crises or needs of others?
3. How do you handle these situations?
4. What do you do to make sure others know you are focusing on an important task?
5. What have you done to help your team focus on priorities?

Making Goal

A little league baseball team plays most of its games in the park across from my home. I like to watch the seven and eight-year olds because most of them are not really sure what to do. Sometimes they forget to watch the game or they play with bugs in the grass.

It all comes together though, when they hit or catch a ball.

One little guy lived in the outfield. He would pound his glove, hitch up his pants and wait for something to happen. Every once in a while a ball would come his way. Then, he would thrust out his glove and run in circles under the approaching ball. Twice I saw him connect.

Each time he looked over at his coach with a smile of satisfaction on his face. When the coach yelled, "Way to go Ernie," I'm certain little Ernie felt a small thrill at having achieved success.

One way to motivate people is to help them set goals and work to achieve them. As they experience small steps of success, your words of encouragement will help them maintain their enthusiasm. Once people get turned on to the positive feelings that come from achieving goals, they want to repeat their success to recreate that feeling.

Application Questions

1. How often do you use praise, compliments and recognition with your team?
2. Why is it important to tie it to a specific part of an employee's performance rather than just complimenting in general?
3. How important is it to give that recognition as soon after the event as possible?
4. Should everyone get praise? If not, who should you target? Why?
5. How often do you receive recognition for a job well done?

Black Box Managers

It can be very frustrating working for a Black Box Manager. This is the kind of manager who isn't really sure what he wants and depends on you to figure it out for him. He says things like, "I need you to work up a plan for increasing our market share for the rest of the year." If you ask him for more specifics or parameters for this plan, he waves you away saying he is sure you can do the job.

You agonize over what this plan should include. You write and re-write. Finally, you take it to your boss. He reads it over and says something like, "Frankly, I am disappointed. I expected more specifics, more detail. In your next draft give me more detail."

You say, thinking you are being really subtle, "Do you want that increase in market share inclusive of just what our unit can do with the main product line or all products?" You hope his response will give you at least an idea of what direction to take.

"Well, what do you think?" is his answer.

This goes on and on, draft after draft. Each time it is like putting your hand in a box and trying to guess by touch what that round thing is inside. Is it a tennis ball? No. Is it a golf ball? No. How about a polo ball? Yes!

How much more effective it is, to have a manager admit they're in need of some ideas and would like to have the benefit of an employee's assistance and help in putting together a plan.

Having others do your thinking for you is dangerous. They just might 'think' you out of a job.

Application Questions

1. What have you done to prevent yourself from operating in a fog?
2. What are some of the hidden costs to working this way?
3. How can giving the other person several options for how a report or project can be drafted help you to get better control over the direction to take?
4. Should reviews be only at the end or throughout to enable you to make mid-course corrections?
5. If you could get the assignment in writing, would that be helpful to both of you?

Slot Machine Management

The fascination of the slot machine is in waiting to see if you've 'won' when you pull the lever. Lights flash, bells sound and the cascade of coins flows from the machine. It is very seductive. If you didn't win that time, maybe you will the next!

The slot machine approach to management is never a win, no matter what. When managers, searching for the magic bullet that will create a dynamic sales team or a streamlined processing operation, try one popular management fad after another, they are behaving like a little old lady in the casino with her bag of nickels.

The only way to know if a change works is to give it time to work! Constant change, hoping for a win, merely leads to confusion and usually lower productivity and results.

Application Questions
1. What management 'fads' have you tried?
2. Did they make a measurable difference?
3. For how long?
4. How did they change your behavior, your team's behavior?

The No-Win Memo

As the manager entered the office, the team was huddled around the department secretary's desk, talking agitatedly. The secretary was holding a memo in one hand and wiping her eyes on a Kleenex with the other.

"I don't know what to do," the secretary moaned.

It seemed that once again, the head of operations had sent another itemized memo of everything that was wrong with yesterday's executive luncheon meeting. The pencils were not aligned at right angles to the reports, the water carafes were 'sweating' on their saucers, the tomatoes were not ripe enough, the bread was 'too fresh', the salad tongs should have been metal, not plastic. A total of 14 improvements were expected for the next meeting.

Every month, the same type of memo appeared no matter how hard everyone tried to make the meeting perfect. It seemed that the small details were more important than the content and purpose of the meeting.

The secretary's manager realized how demoralizing these memos were. She took a red pen and ticked off all the items that related to their caterer. Then she told the secretary to contact the caterer to make the required changes. For the remaining three items on the list, she said, "These are ours to fix. Diane, draft a memo for me to sign, telling our boss we will take care of these three items and we have notified the caterer of the changes they are responsible for." With that she crumpled the memo into a ball and threw it into the wastebasket saying, "Alright, that's our goal for next month, fixing the three items we can fix. Any questions?"

Look at the feedback you give others. Is it usually in the form of criticism? Does it focus on the trivial rather than the important? If so, stop doing that and make some changes. Emphasize what was done well. Make your 'corrective suggestions' around what is important. Your people will respond better and be more enthusiastic about trying to do well.

Application Questions
1. What kind of feedback do you receive from your boss? (positive, negative, very little, none)
2. What kind of feedback do you tend to give your team members? (positive, negative, very little, none)
3. Do you think beginning feedback with what was done well and then explaining how some 'recommended changes' would further improve the overall results would be most effective? Why?
4. If there are a number of improvements needed, would it be more effective if you focused on just one or two at a time? Why?

Rubber Stamp Recognition

After a management session on feedback and coaching, a manager told me he had a 'really good way' of giving his people feedback. He said he had purchased rubber smiling and frowning face stamps. He simply stamped their work with the right rubber stamp.

When I asked him what kind of reaction he was getting to the stamps, he said, "Well nothing has really been said, but it saves me time and they are getting feedback."

If you don't care enough to offer your own specific comments on the quality of what your people produce, don't be surprised if they start putting as much effort into their work as you do in using a rubber stamp.

Application Questions
1. Is feedback such as, "good job" very helpful?
2. When you give feedback, do you take the time to explain 'what' was done well or needs to improve and why this is important?
3. How often do you observe and give feedback on your team member's performance?
4. If you ask for a written report, do you read it with the employee so it can become a coaching moment?

Managers Are Trainers, Too

Overheard in a department; "Glad you're back from that two-day training session Charlie. How was it?"

"Not bad, the instructor kept it pretty lively. We did a couple of workshops that were worthwhile."

"That's good. Now let's see if we can get the contracts I left on your desk out of the door by this afternoon."

The manager will never know what Charlie learned from the session and he certainly won't be following up to reinforce it.

This is a problem in many companies and it is because the Training Department is often considered responsible for improving the knowledge and skills of the employees and therefore their performance results. Wrong! Why this misconception? Because trainers don't set employee performance goals, they can't observe performance or do coaching on a consistent basis of every employee, nor do they conduct performance evaluation and compensation reviews with the employees. These are the basis for improving employee performance results.

In fact, everything that ensures the employee will improve the use of what was learned is in the hands of the managers. That's right. Managers are the real trainers and coaches of their people. Oh, they should use the Training Department to develop a course or help conduct sessions, but the managers need to set the objectives for the course, they need to lead it and then follow up to see that it is being used and coach when it is not. In addition to teaching basic technical and procedural skills, the real purpose of the Training Department is to help the managers do these jobs.

What happens when managers become responsible for training and coaching their staff? First, everyone becomes clear on what is expected from the training. Second, employees take the training more seriously because their boss is leading it. Thirdly, managers know what is being taught so they can watch for the new behaviors and skills. This enables managers to recognize those who are doing well and coach those who need more help. Finally, performance evaluations become more specific and meaningful to the employee and the manager. The best managers know that training and coaching builds strong teams.

Application Questions
1. How do you currently work with your training department or training vendors?
2. How do you currently involve yourself in the training your team receives?
3. Do you have a training plan for each person, including yourself?
4. Do you observe and measure skill and knowledge gains?
5. How do you include training in your coaching and evaluation?

The Enemy within the Camp

The meeting had ended and once again Sam, the regional manager, walked down the hall exasperated and frustrated over Frank's behavior in the meeting. It seemed that every time the group got together to discuss their plans and actions, Frank found fault after fault. He argued with their plans, their strategies, the direction they were taking. When Sam asked him for his ideas or solutions, Frank had none to give.

Sam had noticed Frank having what looked like confidential talks with some of the individuals in the group and he wondered if he was getting paranoid that Frank was plotting something. It was time to take action. He wheeled around and went to Frank's office.

Frank was on the phone when he entered. After closing the door, he quietly said to Frank, "Get off the phone I want to talk to you."

Frank's eyebrows went up and he mouthed into the phone, "Sam is here, I'll call you back later." Leaning back in his chair, he said, "What's up"?

Without any preamble, Sam said, "Let me put it to you this way. I want you to think of this department as a train. It's on the tracks and its going north. Let me repeat that, it is going north. The train has everything it needs to make the trip to its destination. It's got manpower, equipment, and supplies. It has everything it needs, even if there are obstructions along the way. It can overcome them and continue going north.

"Now, you accepted the ticket to get on this train, and you knew where it was going. If you don't want to go north, there are other trains going east, west and south. But, if you are on this train you will be going north. Do you get my point?"

Frank cleared his throat and replied, "Look, I have just been trying to get people to make sure they are making the best decisions."

"Well, if that is true then this is what I expect you to do in meetings from now on. For anything you find fault with, have a recommendation or a solution; otherwise don't disrupt the meeting. Is that clear?"

Don't tolerate behaviors that are divisive to the team. If someone continues after you have clarified your expectations with them, you should tell them to get off your train.

Application Questions

1. Have you ever had someone disrupt your meeting or have you seen it happen to someone else?
2. What was done to stop it from occurring again?
3. What do you do?
4. What more could you do should it happen in the future?
5. What might you do to prevent such behavior in the first place?

Honest Opinions

A sure way to curb enthusiasm about an idea or a project is to ask employees for honest opinions and then explain to them what is wrong with what they said.

I worked with a client who wanted all of his key people in on all of his ideas. He always said he valued their input and their experience. Yet, every time he conducted a meeting or a conference call to solicit their comments what he really wanted to hear were affirmations of his idea. Since this was his true purpose, over time the people lost interest and simply gave him what he wanted, to the detriment of his business.

When people believe you respect their opinions and are willing to consider them, they will be interested, even enthusiastic to be involved. Who knows, they might provide even better springboards for future developments.

A manager, who was highly respected by her team, told me that she always asked them to find at least three things that were wrong with an idea and at least two things that were good about it. This opened the door for a lively discussion and generated new paths of thinking. It's exciting to turn people on.

Application Questions
1. When do you ask for other people's opinions, ideas, and suggestions?
2. How do you explain to them what you are going to do with what they offer or, don't you do this?
3. If you don't agree with an idea offered, what do you say?
4. Why is it important to treat other ideas and opinions with respect?
5. How do you do this?

Slightly Perfect

The CEO of a large successful insurance company regularly had what he called Mentoring Meetings, with his managers. I asked him for an example of what he covered in one of these meetings.

He said, "I cover reality management. That is, how to manage on your feet every day. Last week we discussed why it's more effective and efficient to carry plans and projects to 80% rather than go for 100%. You want to know why?"

I nodded.

"Well, first of all, it saves costs, second, it saves time and third it means we can have more projects in play at the same time. Last of all, as things are constantly in a state of flux, by the time we got a project to 100%, conditions will have changed anyway."

Being slightly perfect makes perfect sense.

Application Questions
1. Should you shoot for 100% even if you may accept less?
2. Why can perfectionism seem de-moralizing?
3. Changes in which of the following would cause you to accept 80% instead of going forward to 100%?
   - time to complete the project
   - cost overruns
   - proposed changes in materials, technology
   - proposed changes in public policies
   - changes in the economy
   - employee issues

Problem Solving Isn't Having All the Answers

Many managers have a blind spot when it comes to recognizing and solving problems. They generally tend to see only two kinds of problems, those they know how to solve and those that can't be ignored because they have turned into a crisis!

The ones they know how to solve are comfortable old friends. They can resolve these quickly and feel good about them. For those that have reached a state of crisis, they call a general alert and get everybody working on solving it.

The great majority of problems are the ones that fall in between these two types. These problems managers don't see or tend to ignore. The primary reason managers have this blind spot is because when such a problem is called to their attention, they don't know what to do about it. They have no experience to call upon. Most of the time, they hope it will resolve itself.

The manager of a group of computer technicians seemed oblivious to the amount of squabbling going on within the group. It wasn't until two of the group quit and a third was about to leave that he acknowledged he had a problem. When asked why he hadn't done something before, he said, he felt it was 'their' problem and they were adults and should have addressed it themselves. His HR director told him they just had, by quitting.

Smart managers know what is going on in their business and address small problems before they grow into big ones. You don't have to have an answer; you just have to acknowledge the problem and ask questions. Every problem is a chance to learn.

Application Questions

1. What are some of the signals that should tell you that you have a problem?

   - complaints
   - increasing error rates
   - decreasing sales
   - turnaround times
   - morale or communication issues with the team or other departments

2. What do you do to resolve a problem?

3. What else could you do?

4. Is there anything you are doing you should not do because it isn't resulting in solving your problem?

Taking Risks

"Fred, how long has my company been banking with you?"

The bank manager thought for a moment and replied, "I'd say it's been at least 15 years, why?"

Dave Wright said, "It's too bad that after all this time, I'm going to have to close our accounts with you."

Fred's eyes opened wide, eyebrows escalating to his hairline, "Why are you going to do that? Haven't we always given you good service and fair rates on loans?"

"You've treated us fairly, but this policy on returning our checks is not acceptable. Several of my customers are upset with us and I am personally embarrassed."

Fred didn't want to lose one of his best customers. He asked Dave to tell him what had happened to his checks.

"Your bank returned several of the checks we had issued to our customers saying we didn't have enough funds to cover them. Now, you and I both know that, even if we didn't have the funds in one account, we had more than enough funds in other accounts. When I had my CFO talk with your branch manager she told him that it was bank policy to return checks for insufficient funds. I would have expected you to honor the checks and call me to let me know we needed to transfer some money from one account to the other."

After Fred had smoothed things over with Dave Wright, he called the branch manager and told her from now on before she followed 'bank policy', she should check the status of the customer because policies are guidelines not laws and there are going to be exceptions to them.

Many times employees don't want to take the risk of making a mistake or getting in harm's way so they do only what they have been told and nothing more. If you want them to take prudent risk, teach them how. Take your ten most common customer problems and have your employees figure out what they can do that isn't illegal or unethical to solve each one. When they develop competence and confidence with the first ten, tackle the next ten. Your employees will thank you and so will your customers.

Application Questions

1. How do you currently coach your team in resolving customer issues?
2. What do you do to follow up to see if they are applying your coaching correctly?
3. If a team member makes a mistake in judgment, what do you do?
4. Have you ever used "what if" scenarios to test the team's responses to different customer situations? Why would that be beneficial?

The Warm Body Syndrome

Employee selection is a continuing challenge for managers. In most companies, Human Resources screens candidates that supposedly qualify based on job description requirements. However, it is the manager's responsibility to determine which candidate has the right attitude and will fit into the team.

Because this isn't always easy to foretell, sometimes managers fall back on taking the best 'warm body' to fill the gap. Sometimes by sheer serendipity the warm body works out; more often it doesn't and the selection cycle repeats itself.

One way to reduce the risk of poor selection is to consider the weight you give to these aspects of the job; knowledge, skills, attitude and experience. If you put a lot of weight on experience and hire someone who has done the job well for a long time elsewhere, that person may not find enough challenge in the job and expect to be promoted rather quickly.

If you put most of the weight on job knowledge and operational skills your choice may be technically adept, but lack the ability to develop good interpersonal relationships with the team and your customers.

The best fit is the candidate who has a naturally positive, open and inquisitive attitude with enough knowledge, skills and experience to be able, with coaching, to step into the job.

Knowledge and skills continually need to be upgraded. But attitude can only be influenced by the environment you set. So unless someone comes in with the right attitude, they may never be willing to learn what they need to succeed on your team.

Application Questions

1. Thinking back, have you ever had an employee with a bad attitude at work?
2. If so, how did that affect the work, the team and your customers?
3. What are some of the visible signs of a poor or negative attitude?
4. Do you ever display any of these?
5. Why is your attitude important in terms of your team?

Take Two Aspirin and Call Me in the Morning

What would happen if a doctor gave every patient that came to him the same treatment? Oh, he might cure some, but more often he would have a lot of sick patients getting sicker!

The same is true of managers who use the same kind of approach to resolving every employee performance problem. Some managers try to cajole employees to improve. They say, "Come on, you can do it, I know you can." Some try to get employees to determine how to improve themselves. They say, "You know you need to improve. What are you going to do about it?" This is really frustrating because if the employee knew, he would probably be already doing it! Still others use the team to create feelings of guilt. "You know Betty, we're all counting on you, don't let us down!"

Whether it is because employees just don't know what they are supposed to do or they don't know how to do it or they don't feel motivated to do it; as a manager you have to tailor your approach to fit the source of the individual employee's problems.

Lack of understanding means you need to reaffirm their goals and your expectations. Lack of skill requires training and coaching. And since motivation comes from within, managers need to demonstrate that they will help by coaching and supporting any and all efforts to succeed. Managers can shape the employee's behavior and in so doing create a motivating environment.

So, if all you have been doing is doling out the 'aspirin' you may not be using the right approach to treat the different symptoms!

Application Questions

1. If you use the same approach with everyone will it come off as sincere?
2. How do you convey a sense of interest and honestly wanting to help?
3. If you see a bit of improvement what do you do?
4. What changes could you make to be more effective in helping your people improve their performance?
5. When will you make these?

The Delegation Ladder

One of the best ways to develop people is by giving them opportunities to take on more responsibilities. There is a win in this for you, too, because by delegating tasks you free more of your time, which in turn allows you to take on more responsibilities which is something your boss dearly wants you to do.

Now it is a serious mistake to think that delegation is the assigning of the task. When this is all that the manager does, he or she may be in for an unfortunate surprise. The task may not get done well or even done at all. Why is this?

Here is the major problem. When you decide to delegate a task to someone you have to let them know how much authority they have to get the task completed. You can tell them to come to you to discuss the task, and then let them perform the task and report back so you can review what they have done. Or, you can have them perform the task and report back to tell you it's done. Or, you can tell them from now on it's their job to do and there's no need to report back. The amount of authority depends on the knowledge, skills and experience of the employee.

Over time you can move employees up your delegation ladder as they gain experience. Look at the tasks that have been delegated to you. Whenever you didn't know how much authority you had to accomplish them, how frustrating was that for you? Don't repeat that with your people.

Application Questions

1. To truly delegate a task review this list to see if you are including all of these items when you delegate:
   - Why you have chosen them for the task
   - The level of authority they have to complete the task
   - The resources they have to work with
   - The time when it should be completed
   - What success looks like!
2. What tasks can you delegate?
3. What is the value to you of delegating some of your tasks?

Closing the Loop

One way employees gauge what is important is by what their manager takes the time to look at. There's an old truism, "Inspect what you expect, because employees respect what bosses inspect". This is one of the ways employees determine what is important. This helps them set their priorities.

The mere act of setting expectations for what and how employees should perform is not enough. You have to close the loop by observing what is actually being done. Why take the time to do this?

Here are a few reasons managers gave me when I asked them for the benefits of closing the loop.

- Observing helps managers set priorities with employees
- If performance isn't up to standard, it gives the manager a chance to coach for improvement
- Observing clarifies expectations
- It builds stronger teams
- It develops employees
- It helps motivate employees, and
- It gives managers a chance to recognize good performance.

Think about your employees. Are you closing the loop?

Application Questions

1. Are your employees clear about your expectations of them?
2. How do you know for sure?
3. What do you do to determine how well they are performing against your expectations?
4. How often do you follow up?
5. When they are meeting or exceeding your expectations, what do you do?
6. What do you do if they are not meeting expectations?
7. What do you need to change about what you are currently doing in order to help your team maintain or improve their performance?

How Good Is Good?

One of the most important responsibilities of every manager is to evaluate the performance of those who report to them. While managers can use all kinds of numerical systems to arrive at a final evaluation, the reality is that unless they can back the evaluation up with facts, what they are offering is their opinion.

Facts come from observing what the employee does and the results of those actions. The more specific this information is the more valuable the evaluation becomes to the employee because they know the basis on which they are being judged. This tells them either what they need to keep doing or what they need to correct.

Another benefit is that employees tend to respect managers who provide them with facts. They know the manager is aware of what they have done and interested in how they perform.

Which would you rather hear? "Bob, you're doing a good job. Overall, I'm giving you a satisfactory for this year." Or, "Bob, you have made a steady improvement in your performance. In fact compared to last year, you increased your sales volume by 8%. I have observed that you sound more confident explaining our products, especially to the older customers. I have read two positive customer letters in which they mentioned you by name as being very helpful. Based on your customer service and your sales results, you have earned a satisfactory rating for the year."

As they say, the devil is in the details.

Application Questions
1. What kind of notes or coaching logs do you keep on your employees?
2. How often do you spend time observing and reviewing your employees' performance?
3. What kind of preparation do you make when you plan to conduct a performance evaluation?
4. How do you involve your employee in their evaluation?
5. What could you do to improve the effectiveness of your evaluations?

The A Virus

An immense amount of research has been done on the 'A' Virus. Here are the primary facts. First, everyone has it. Second, it cannot be eliminated or eradicated; however it can mutate. And that last point is an extremely important fact.

As a doctor would say, let's take a look at two ways the virus can present itself by observing two people doing the same type of work. Let's say these people are tellers or bank cashiers in two different banks. The first has a line of people waiting to be served. It's late in the afternoon and she is tired. She is dealing with a man who is complaining about the long wait he has had. She looks at the man and says, "Look, I'm not paid to listen to your complaints. If you would learn to use the ATM you wouldn't have to wait!"

The second person has also had a long day. She has several customers who have been waiting a while because she has been dealing with an elderly woman who doesn't understand how she could be overdrawn. After explaining several times, this teller announces to those in her line; "I'm going to walk Mrs. Prentiss over to one of our bankers. I'll be right back to take care of you. Thank you for your patience."

Each of them has the Attitude Virus. The difference is one has the positive and the other, the negative version. Even though each of us is responsible for our attitude, being in a positive environment tends to help negative attitudes mutate into positive ones.

Managers can help create positive environments by modeling positive attitudes themselves because this sets up the conditions in which others can 'catch' the positive Attitude Virus. Good feelings tend to be contagious.

Application Questions

1. What do others say and do to project the kind of attitude they have?
2. What behaviors and actions do you do to display a positive, upbeat attitude?
3. When you are feeling down, what do you do to prevent it from coloring your attitude?
4. When one of your team shows a negative attitude to their customers or peers, what do you do about it?
5. What else could you do?

It's Curtains for Customer Service

Every business talks a good game about customer service. They produce countless versions of the phrase, 'We're here to Serve You' as part of commercials and advertisements. Yet, reality falls far below the expectations the businesses have set for themselves.

Here's a case in point heard at a national conference on business practices. A speaker recounted how she had ordered drapes from a nationally known department store. The store explained they needed to order the fabric and that it would take about three months for the drapes to be completed. They would call her when they were ready. Three months passed, four months passed. She called the drapery workroom and was told the fabric had come in flawed and they had sent for more. They would be ready in a month. A month passed. She called again and was told that they were backed up with orders, but would get to hers within two weeks. Two weeks passed. She called again and was told it would be another two weeks.

The speaker said she decided to bypass the workroom and go straight to the store president. She called the store's general number and asked for the name of their president. Armed with the name, she called back and asked for Mr. White's office. When his secretary answered, she said, "This is Mrs. Smith, returning Mr. White's call. The secretary put her through. When she got him on the phone, she explained that she was a very angry customer and expected him to do something about the terrible customer service she had received from the drapery department. He listened and then told her to call the workroom at 9:00 the next morning and they would be sure to satisfy her.

At 9:00 she called the drapery workroom. The supervisor was waiting for her call. "Mrs. Smith, I am watching your drapes being sewn together at this very minute." Mrs. Smith replied, "You mean the panels have been cut and they are in the process of sewing them?"

"Yes," the supervisor said.

"Fine, then cancel my order. You see it's the principle of the thing to me. You weren't interested in me as the customer. It was only when I got your bosses involved that you did anything. I would never enjoy those drapes now."

That's the thing about customers. We don't like to be diddled with!

Application Questions

1. Who are your customers? Are they other departments? Are they external customers? Are they both?
2. What standards for customer service have you set?
3. How do you measure the quality of service you provide?
4. How important is it for your level of customer service to be consistent? Why?
5. What are three things you could do to improve the quality of customer service your team provides?

Different Strokes

An executive once complained that he was really disappointed that his new sales person hadn't increased his sales much even though he had been to a high-powered sales training seminar. I told him that was like saying you could play a great game of golf after spending the weekend on the driving range.

You see, even if you get outstanding at driving the ball, that isn't going to equip you to know how to use the right club to hit over water, out of the rough, out of the sand trap, pitch onto the green and putt into the hole. Learning all those strokes takes coaching and practice.

The next time someone comes back from a sales training course, start coaching them on how to apply what they learned in many of the different situations you know they will encounter. That's the way they improve their game.

Application Questions
1. What actions and behaviors do you currently coach your team on?
2. Is your coaching both one-on-one and as a group?
3. Do you practice different sales and service situations with your team? Why should you?
4. If you could improve three things you do in coaching, what would they be?
5. What are the two most important areas your team needs to improve in? Are you coaching on these now?

True Team Power

The same factors tend to be prevalent in most successful teams. They have a common vision or goal, they all contribute their experience and skills and they practice, practice, practice. They all are visibly involved in helping the team move ahead.

Coaches and managers are integral to their team's success because they focus on watching everyone perform, they give constructive suggestions and they recognize individual and team improvements continually. These managers understand that people get bogged down by the pressure of work and the repetition and familiarity of activities can dull their performance. That's why it is important that the manager uses their progress against goal to keep the team focused.

Gifted managers do things to add a sense of fun and competition to work. One such manager had a dart board in the employee break room. The first person to hit their quota for the day got to throw three darts at balloons pinned on the board. If they hit one, they got the prize hidden in the balloon. Prizes were things like leaving work two hours early one day, or babysitting money for one night out, or a coupon for free dry cleaning. Another manager held a barbeque for her team when they achieved their goals.

One bank branch manager wanted her team to improve their product knowledge. She asked them for ideas on how to get more time to practice without taking time away from serving their customers. One of the team suggested they get the customers involved. They created a deck of cards containing product knowledge questions. Every team member had a deck of the cards with a small sign requesting customers to take one and ask their banker the question. So all day long everyone practiced and the customers got a kick out of helping. The team increased their product knowledge, they sold more products, and the customers had fun, too.

Managers don't have to be creative in a vacuum. They can get their team involved in designing ways to help themselves! Now, that's true involvement and teamwork.

Application Questions
1. How do you get your people motivated to achieve?
2. How do you involve your people in building their team?
3. What kinds of activities have you used to liven up your team?
4. If someone is not contributing to the team, what do you do?
5. What could you do more of to improve teamwork?

Merging Managers

More attention is paid to administrative and operational aspects of an acquisition than is paid to the employees involved. This is one reason why many acquisitions are not as successful as expected. Here is what happens with the employees in many acquisitions. The acquiring company sends their Human Resource Managers to tell them they will be interviewed and once the interviews are over, those that will be retained will be informed. Some companies show a video extolling how wonderful the acquiring company is. There is a question and answer period addressing general benefit questions and the meeting is over. Employees leave filled with uncertainty, +concern and even fear about their future.

One Southern bank after purchasing several small banks, realized that they needed to do more because the local communities were hearing negative comments about them after these initial meetings. In their next acquisition, they set up a bank fair in the local hotel ballroom. Departments representing all areas of the bank put up booths to 'sell' what their department did to the acquired employees. As these employees visited the booths they were greeted and told how the areas supported the bank and the community. Investment Representatives dressed up in tuxedos and served ginger ale in plastic champagne glasses as they talked about helping make their customers' money. Retail dressed up as doctors and did 'financial check-ups' on the employees. The Training Department, dressed as chefs, passed out recipes made up of employee training courses.

What was the result? This people-focused approach gained great receptivity and relations between the two institutions was off to a better start.

Another organization selected a number of top performing offices and had the managers from the acquired institution spend 30 days working in these branches in rotating shifts so they would get a better sense of the operational aspects as well as the corporate culture.

Get the people on your side and resistance is lowered.

Application Questions
1. Have you been involved in an acquisition?
2. If so, what went well? What could have been done differently to improve the results?
3. Could any of this be applied to newly acquired employees?

Passing the Baton

Change and reorganization have always been with us. Lately, the pace of both seems to be accelerating. This is true of all businesses globally. We read about it daily as it currently impacts the automotive, steel, and related products industries. We see it on the news as we listen to commentators talk about the banking industry. This isn't going to stop and managers need to find ways to help themselves and their teams to assimilate these changes.

A human resource manager in a large East Coast corporation told me that one of the things they did was use transition meetings whenever department managers were changed. The purpose of this meeting was for the exiting manager to thank the team for their efforts and give a brief review of their successes. The exiting manager also introduced the new manager, giving a little of his or her background and what he or she was bringing to the team.

The new manager talked about his or her management style, how they liked to communicate and their expectations for the immediate quarter. There was an informal question and answer period and a schedule for individual meetings was made up so the new manager could meet with each team member to determine their individual expertise, strengths and skills. This was important because often the new manager was not experienced in the operations of the business unit and would need to draw upon the capabilities inherent in the team members.

Did this mean there were no problems and everyone got along well? No, it just meant 'passing the baton' this way upped the odds in favor of teams getting off to a better start.

Application Questions

1. What are the pros and cons of rotating managers?
2. What preparation should you do before meeting your new team?
3. What are the critical pieces of information you would need to know in order to make a smooth transition to a new team?
4. What would you want the new team to know about you in order to work best with you?